Maria Wiesmüller

AUSTRIAN
SPECIALTIES

 Kitchen Delights

Before you begin!

Austria is popular year 'round because of its lovely landscapes and innumerable sights. Austrian cuisine is famed and admired far beyond its borders. It covers a broad spectrum of regional specialties from Austria's nine provinces.

Many famous dishes are also legacies of the Austro-Hungarian monarchy and have their origins in Bohemia, Hungary or Croatia. Some have been refined over the years, or today are made with different ingredients. The recipes in this book provide an impression of the delicious variety offered by Austria's cuisines. You will find recipes for sophisticated soups, a variety of appetizers, as well as entrées famous all over the world, like the ever-popular "Wiener Schnitzel" or "Steirisches Wurzelfleisch" (Styrian Root Vegetable Stew).

Of course, hearty, home-style dishes also form an integral part of Austrian cuisine.

The final pages of this book are devoted to Austrian desserts and sweet dishes, with many recipes for famous pastries and magnificent tortes.

The easy-to-follow recipes and mouth-watering color photographs will delight your whole family.

Because most Europeans weigh their ingredients rather than measure them in cups and ounces, a food scale is recommended for these recipes.

The following introduction provides interesting facts and information about Austria's regional diversity.

I hope you enjoy my culinary tour through Austria and wish you much success and fun while trying out these recipes! Guten Appetit!

Sincerely,

Maria Wiesmüller

Austrian Cuisine – Region for Region

BURGENLAND, Austria's easternmost province, was once part of Hungary and has only belonged to the Republic of Austria since 1921. Many Burgenland dishes have been influenced by Hungarian cuisine, with its abundant use of paprika, cabbage, lard, as well as the ever-popular goulash (gulyas). Other well-known and delicious dishes include Garlic Soup, Cabbage Strudel and "Schöberln," or fruit fritters.

CARINTHIA is Austria's southernmost, and therefore sunniest, province. Here we find dishes based on different types of grains, combined with meats or dairy products. Typical specialties are "Kasnudeln" (Carinthian Cheese Pastries), "Kirschmandeltascherln" (Cherry Pockets) and Stuffed Pork Rib Roast. A perfect accompaniment for the last dish is "Trenten," a dark wheat or rye roll. The cuisine of Austria's largest province is as diverse as its ever-changing landscape of mountains, lakes and meadows.

LOWER AUSTRIA. Almost each region boasts its own specialty. Lower Austria's proximity to Bohemia and Hungary and to the major European trade routes - the "Salt Road" and the "Wine Road" - has had a significant influence on the region's food to this day. Lower Austria's

vintners, Danube River fishermen and the vegetable growers of the bountiful "Marchfeld" region have made significant contributions to the multifaceted cuisine.

Smoked Pork, Deep-Fried Danube Carp and Poppy Seed Dumplings are only a sample of what this region offers. Potatoes play a major role in Lower Austria's cooking. Even though one of its regions, the "Waldviertel" (or Forest Region), has a somewhat raw climate, it produces some of Austria's largest potatoes. All types of strudels are popular here, as are yeast breads, pastries and dumplings. The Wachau Apricot Dumplings deserve particular mention, and Lower Austrian "Powidltascherln," delicate pockets with prune filling, originated in Bohemia, the province's northern neighbor.

UPPER AUSTRIA is also known for its hearty, home-style dishes. "Eating and drinking are what keep body and soul intact" is a favorite motto here. All-time favorites are the many different types of dumplings, served with a crispy pork roast or in a tasty broth. One hearty specialty from the "Mühlviertel" (Mill Region) is potato dumplings filled with chopped roast or cooked meats known as "Mühlviertler G'hackknödel." The Linzer Torte's fame has spread far beyond provincial borders. At Christmas time, many places offer "Kletzenbrot," a dark fruitbread made with dried pears ("Kletzen"), candied fruits, nuts and spices like cinnamon, cloves and anise.

When you think of SALZBURG, you probably think of the renowned "Salzburger Nockerln," a sweet soufflé of egg whites, sugar and a touch of flour. In addition to its meat dishes, Salzburg's cuisine is also known for its broad range of yeast pastries, most of which are either baked or deep-fried. The Mozart Torte, a sweet-tooth's dream come true, is certainly one of this region's most well known pastries.

STYRIA, Austria's second largest province, is known as "Austria's Heart of Green" because of its vast, lush forests. Old history books from this region reveal a number of interesting cooking habits, such as the northwest Styrian custom of cooking primarily on top of the stove, rather than in the oven. For this reason, many foods are simmered or deep-fried in lard or oil. By contrast, most dishes prepared in southeastern Styria are baked. Today, Styria's cuisine is known for its Wine Soup and its famous Root Vegetable Stew ("Wurzelfleisch"). Austria's trademark "Guglhupf," a delightful coffee ring and typically Austrian pastry, probably had its origins here. The cuisine of mountainous **TYROL** is largely influenced by its close proximity to Italy, as well as by recipes and techniques passed down from the reign of Emperor Maximilian. Hearty, filling dishes are the mainstay of this region's specialties.

"Gerscht," or Tyrolean Barley Soup, is as satisfying and nutritional as "Tiroler Gröstl," a savory fried potato and meat dish, or "Speckknödel," bread dumplings with bacon. Throughout Tyrol, you will find every sort of sweet or savory fried dumpling ("Krapfen") as well.

Austria's westernmost, and smallest, province is **VORARLBERG.** Its cuisine is characterized by the generous use of milk and cheese in preparing many of its dishes. "Kässpätzle," or Vorarlberg Cheese Spaetzle, and Bread Soup, along with several delicious stews, are the trademarks of this Alpine region. Its tasty cheeses have also made the province famous throughout Austria. After a meal, Vorarlberg's natives enjoy a "Zwätchger" (plum brandy) or a "Kriesner" (cherry brandy), made of flavorful mountain cherries.

Down through the centuries Austria's capital city, **VIENNA,** became the center of a richly diversified, very ethnic cuisine. Viennese cuisine, known all over the world, is characterized by its clear soups with a variety of additions, its diverse breaded and fried dishes like the perennial "Wiener Schnitzel" and Viennese Fried Chicken ("Backhendl"), as well as its many braised meat dishes.

A cookbook of Austrian specialties would not be complete without mentioning the broad array of desserts

and pastries, like "Kaiser-schmarrn" (Emperor's Pancake), Apple Strudel and naturally, the Sacher Torte. Coffee in any variation, with a tender "Kipferl" (crescent roll) and the Viennese coffeehouse are important players in the cuisine of this world-famous city. A closer view of the many delicious coffee beverages is provided after the recipes.

AUSTRIAN WINE PRIMER

When you think about Vienna, you will also probably think about a wonderful evening in one of the many **"Heuriger"** wine taverns serving the year's new wine. The word "Heuriger" (pronounced hoy-rigger) is somewhat confusing, since it is used to designate both the locale where you can enjoy the new wine, as well as the young wine itself. Actually, "Heuriger" wine is made from the most recent grape harvest and earns its name for one year starting on St. Martin's Day, November 11. A cluster of evergreen twigs bound tightly to a pole and hung in front of a locale signals that "Heuriger" wine is being served.

A genuine Heuriger host serves only wine produced from grapes grown in his own vineyards. The full-bodied wines from Nussberg or Kahlenberg, or the fresh-fruity ones from Bisamberg, wine-growing regions around

Vienna, are lovingly called "three-quarter time" wines, ones that make the hearts of true wine connoisseurs beat to the Viennese waltz.

Vienna is located in the midst of excellent wine-growing districts, like Klosterneuburg and Gumpoldskirchen, which along with Krems, Langenlois, the Wachau, Retz and Vöslau comprise Austria's largest wine producing region. The classic white wine of this province is the fruity, peppery "Grüner Veltliner," a wine unique to Austria with grapes ripened on the sun-drenched glacial slopes that skirt the Danube River.

In Burgenland, Austria's second largest wine-producing region, excellent red and white wines are made of grapes ripened in the Pannonian climate. The main wine district is found on the gentle shores of Lake Neusiedel. Rust, with its lovely Old Town, is counted among Austria's most beautiful cities and was declared a Model City by the European Council in 1975. Wine-lovers should not miss the opportunity to taste the full, fruity "Blau-fränkisch" red wine, which,

like the "St. Laurent," "Traminer" and "Muskat-Ottonel" wines, are made of grapes that flourish in the climate and soils of Burgenland.

Wine has been part of Styria's history since Celtic times. Schilcher, a distinct rosé, is probably the most well-known of this region's wines, especially because of its delicate color. A Styrian specialty, Schilcher has a fresh taste with low acidity and is produced from the blue Wildbach grape, which grows in western Styria around Deutschlandsberg and Stainz. Should you visit this part of Austria, be sure to see one of the most delightful spots on earth, Southern Styria and the ancient settlement of Leibnitz. Kitzeck, Europe's highest wine-growing community, offers a magnificent panorama of the Styrian wine-growing district. The most widely grown wine grape in Styria is the Welschriesling, followed by Müller-Thurgau and sauvignon blanc (Muskat-Sylvaner) grapes. Another popular Styrian wine is the Gewürztraminer from the vineyards of Klöch in eastern Styria.

East Tyrolean Barley Soup/
Osttiroler Gerstensuppe

• Rinse pearl barley with cold water. Soak in cold water overnight. Finely dice the bacon and slowly brown in a large skillet or pot. Drain pearl barley, add to pot and fry with the browned bacon. Add part of the broth and simmer.

• Peel and finely dice the onions. Wash, peel and julienne cut carrots, celery root and leek. Add vegetables and onions to the bacon/barley mixture and add remaining broth. Add salt and pepper to taste. Bring to a boil, then reduce heat. Simmer for approximately two hours, or until barley is tender.

One-half hour before serving,

3 oz barley	
5 oz bacon	
6 cups (2 1/2 pts) beef stock	
2 small onions	
2 carrots	
1 large leek	
2 medium potatoes	
salt, white pepper	
pinch of nutmeg	
1 T flour	
cold water	
2 T sour cream	
4 thin slices of crisp bacon	

Serve with dark rye bread

add finely diced potatoes to the soup. Slowly brown bacon strips until crisp. Ten minutes prior to serving, mix flour with cold water in a cup and add to soup to thicken. Correct the seasoning, add grated nutmeg and stir in sour cream. Do not boil soup after adding cream. Garnish soup with crisp bacon strips when serving.

Our tip:

Barley soup is very popular among the entire mountain-dwelling populace of Austria, since barley grows well even at high altitudes (1500 m - 1700 m). Made without meat it was a favorite at Lent, served with onions browned in butter.

Fried Semolina Dumpling Soup/ Gebackene Griessknödelsuppe

Upper Austria

2 oz softened butter

2 eggs

5 T semolina

2 T sour cream

shortening

4 cups (32 oz) clear beef stock

salt, pepper

2 T chives, finely chopped

• Beat butter until creamy. Stir in eggs, semolina and salt. Let stand for approximately 20 min. Form small 1 1/2-inch dumplings (scoop up dough and roll between palms to form balls).

• Melt shortening in a deep frying pan. Add dumplings and fry until golden brown, turning constantly. Remove and drain on paper towel. Heat broth, add fried dumplings and bring to a boil. Correct seasoning. Garnish with chopped chives.

Garlic Soup/ Knoblauchsuppe

Burgenland

7 oz mixed vegetables (1 carrot, 1 celery stick, 1 small leek, parsley)

2 T butter

salt, pepper

2 oz butter or shortening

1 - 2 medium onions, chopped

3 - 5 garlic cloves, crushed

pinch of ground ginger, caraway

2 T flour

5 cups (2 pts) beef stock

• Finely chop soup vegetables (carrots, parsley root, celery, leek). Melt butter and sauté vegetables until tender. Add seasonings and broth. Bring to a boil. Reduce heat and simmer for about 20 min. Put the soup mixture into a blender and blend until smooth.

• Melt the shortening. Sauté onion and garlic until translucent. Season with ground ginger. Stir in flour to form a roux. Reheat soup and add flour mixture to soup. Season to taste. Serve hot.

13

Bread Soup/Geröstete Brotsuppe

Vorarlberg

• Cut bread into cubes or very thin slices. Peel and finely chop onions. Wash, dry and finely chop parsley.

• Combine these ingredients with flour; slowly brown in melted shortening or butter, stirring constantly.

• Add broth and water. Season. Simmer until bread is soft. Pour soup mixture into a blender, blend until smooth. Return to pot.

• Beat eggs, whipping cream and pinch of nutmeg. Add to soup to thicken. Garnish with caraway, crushed garlic to taste and toasted bread slices or croutons. Serve immediately.

| 5 oz dried dark rye bread |
| 1 large onion |
| 2 T parsley, finely chopped |
| 2 T flour |
| approx. 2 oz butter or shortening |
| 2 cups (3/4 pt) water |
| 2 cups (3/4 pt) beef stock |
| salt, white pepper |
| 1 - 2 eggs |
| 2 T cream |
| pinch of nutmeg |
| pinch of ground caraway |
| 1 garlic clove, crushed (optional) |

Our Tip:

To make this soup even more interesting, you can add cooked sliced carrots, thinly sliced sausage or frankfurters, or diced ham.

If you use dried white bread instead of dark rye, you will be making a "Panadlsuppe." All other ingredients remain the same. Bread soups are also very popular in Styria, although in that region boiled or roasted meat is added, along with several lemon fillets. Styrian cooks also mix 1 or 2 egg yolks with 2 T of sour cream, which they then drizzle over the pieces of meat floating on the soup. To give the soup a golden-brown crust, place the soup dishes in a hot oven (or broiler) just before serving.

15

Wine Soup/
Weinsuppe Styria

3 - 5 slices of dried white bread **or** 3 - 5 dried white rolls

2 - 3 T butter

1 tsp ground cinnamon

4 cups (1 3/4 pt) white wine

4 - 5 T sugar

grated rind of 1 lemon

6 - 8 egg yolks, beaten

4 T sour cream

• Cut bread into cubes, brown in butter and sprinkle with cinnamon. Put aside.

• Bring white wine to a boil, add sugar and grated lemon rind. Reduce heat. Combine egg yolks and cream. Beat slowly into wine with a wire whisk. Serve soup topped with cinnamon croutons.

Stuffed Tomatoes/
Gefüllte Paradeiser

4 large, firm tomatoes	• Wash tomatoes, cut off top and scoop out meat and seeds. Chop ham or sausage and combine with canned corn, peas and chopped pickles.
7 oz (3/4 cup) ham or sausage, chopped	
1 pickle, diced	
1 T parsley, finely chopped	
1 - 2 T corn and peas, precooked	
2 T mayonnaise	• Mix mayonnaise, plain yoghurt and mustard. Season to taste and add to vegetable mixture. Fill tomatoes and serve cold.
1 T yogurt	
1/4 tsp mustard	
salt, white pepper	

Deep-Fried Vegetables/ Gebackenes Gemüse

approx. 2 lbs fresh vegetables (mushrooms, carrots, celery, green beans, cauliflower, broccoli)

8 cups (approx. 4 pts) water

salt

juice of 2 lemons

2 T vinegar

1 tsp sugar

Batter:

11 oz (1 1/4 cups) flour

pinch of salt

3 T oil

4 egg yolks

4 egg whites

approx. 1 1/4 cups (1/2 pt) liquid (e.g. beer, white wine, milk or water)

16 oz (1 lb) shortening **or** 2 1/2 cups (1 pt) vegetable oil

• Clean and dry all vegetables. Cut into bite-sized pieces and florets (cauliflower and broccoli); leave green beans whole. Peel and thinly slice carrots and celery root. In a large pot, bring water to a boil, adding salt, lemon juice, vinegar and sugar.

• Use a wire basket to blanch vegetables in the boiling water. Remove and immediately plunge vegetables into ice water; let drip dry.

• Batter: Mix flour, salt, oil, egg yolks and liquid until smooth. The batter should be thick to ensure that vegetables are fully coated. Let batter stand for about half an hour. Just before using, beat egg whites until stiff and fold into batter.

• Heat oil or shortening. Draw each piece of vegetable individually through the batter and fry until golden brown. Drain on paper towel. Keep hot until ready to serve.

Serve with French or Italian bread.

Tyrolean-Style Potato Salad/
Erdäpfelsalat Tiroler Art

16 oz (2 cans) salad potatoes	black pepper
2 oz smoked bacon in slices	pinch of sugar
1 medium onion	1 tsp drained capers
2 T oil	1 T chives, finely chopped
1 1/2 T wine vinegar	
1 tsp mustard (German mustard)	• Boil salad potatoes until tender. Drain and let cool to manageable temperature. Peel potatoes. Slice still-warm, peeled potatoes into a large
1/2 cup (4 oz) beef stock	
salt	

bowl. Finely dice smoked bacon. Peel and finely chop onions.

• Fry bacon and onions in oil at medium heat until translucent, stirring constantly. Add vinegar to hot pan and stir. Pour mixture over potatoes.

• Warm broth, stir in mustard and add to potatoes. Season strongly with salt and pepper and mix well. Serve with lots of chopped chives.

Our tip:
Tyrolean Potato Salad is an ideal accompaniment to breaded, fried entrées like Wiener Schnitzel (p. 30), Viennese Fried Chicken (p. 44), as well as Fried Carp (p. 46).

F.Y.I.
In Tyrol this potato salad is also mixed with cress, endive lettuce leaves, sliced cucumber, tomatoes, or lamb's lettuce. Potatoes, prepared in a delightful variety of ways, are particularly popular in this province. In many places, they have replaced traditional dishes made with such staples as lentils, beans and peas.

Viennese Potato Salad is also well known in eastern Austria, where it is made without diced bacon. A small, yellow, almost waxy potato from that region, known as the "Kipfler," is particularly suited for such salads.

Boiled Beef with Apple-Horse-radish/ Tafelspitz mit Apfelkren

approx. 2 lbs of beef bones

4 1/2 lbs loin of beef or beef brisket

1 small parsley root, coarsely chopped

1 - 2 carrots, coarsely chopped

2 celery sticks, coarsely chopped

1 small leek

2 garlic cloves, crushed

2 small onions

1 bay leaf

3 T chives, finely chopped

pinch of nutmeg

salt

Sauce:

2 medium apples

2 T wine vinegar

2 - 3 T grated horseradish

1 - 2 tsp sugar

pinch of salt, white pepper

• Rinse beef soup bones and place in a large pot. Cover with water, add salt and bring to a boil. Add beef. Bring to a boil and skim the liquid, several times if necessary. Reduce heat.

• Meanwhile, clean, peel (if necessary) and coarsely chop parsley root, carrots, celery root and leek. Peel and quarter onions and garlic cloves. Add vegetables, bay leaf and salt to soup. Again, bring to a boil and skim.

22

• Simmer in covered pot for about 2 hours, or until beef can be easily pierced with a sharp knife point. During the last half hour before serving, prepare apple-horseradish. Peel, seed and grate apples. Place in a small pot, add vinegar, sugar and cook over low heat for 10-12 min. Let cool. Stir in finely grated horseradish and season to taste.

• Clean and chop chives. Remove meat to a heated serving platter. Strain stock through a fine sieve and add a pinch of nutmeg and salt to taste. Slice meat across the grain and pour a little of the stock over it. Garnish with chives and boiled vegetables, if desired.

Serve with apple horseradish and potatoes.

Veal Birds /Kalbsvögerl

Upper Austria

4 - 6 slices of veal

salt

white pepper

2 oz bacon (or bard)

4 oz ground meat

4 T cream

1 egg yolk, beaten

1 medium onion, chopped

pinch of thyme

1 garlic clove, crushed

1 small onion, chopped

3 oz bacon, diced

stewed vegetables, approx. 3 oz

approx. 1 cup (8 oz) meat stock

Sauce:

1/2 cup (4 oz) sour cream

1 - 2 T flour

approx. 4 oz cooked mushrooms

• Trim the edges of 1/2-inch thick veal slices, rinse and dry. Pound the meat with a cleaver, rub with salt and pepper. Make the filling as follows: Finely chop bacon and sauté until golden brown; combine with ground meat in a bowl. Add cream, 1/2 the chopped onions, egg yolk, steamed vegetables, thyme and crushed garlic. Spread a thin layer of filling on each slice of meat. Roll the meat; secure with skewers or thread.

• Dredge the birds in flour. Sauté remaining onions with diced bacon. Then sauté the birds in the onion/bacon mixture until golden brown. Add stock and reduce heat. Cover and simmer for 40-50 min., until tender.

• Remove the birds; remove skewers or thread.

• To make pan gravy: Add flour to sour cream and stir until smooth. Add to pan juices and bring to a boil. Add mushrooms. Correct seasoning. Return birds to gravy for several minutes. Serve immediately.

F.Y.I.

Well into the 19th century, song birds, particularly larks, were popularly prepared in this fashion in many of Upper Austria's larger cities. "Bird-catchers" delivered the birds to wealthier households. These delicious veal birds were prepared by those who could not afford the "real thing."

Steak and Onions/ Zwiebelrostbraten

Vienna

2 medium onions	
2 T flour	
4 sirloin steaks, approx. 7 oz each	
salt	
white pepper	
5 T oil	
1/2 cup (4 oz) beef stock	
1 T butter	
4 small pickles (garnish)	

• Peel onions and cut into thin rings. Heat butter in a small frying pan and sauté the onion rings at medium heat until they are a crisp golden brown. Remove from heat and set aside. Remove onion rings and place on a plate. Keep warm.

• Rinse steaks under cold water, dry with paper towel and pound flat with a cleaver. Rub both sides of meat with salt and pepper. While doing this, heat oil in a large, heavy skillet.

• Put flour on a flat plate. Dip one side of meat in flour, shake to remove excess and place in oil, floured side down. Sauté meat, allowing 4-6 min. per side. Meat should still be somewhat pink inside (medium).

• Remove steaks to a warmed serving platter. Add broth to skillet in which steaks were cooked and bring to a boil (you can also add butter remaining from the onions, if you wish). Season to taste. Pour over steaks.

• Add onion rings to steaks. Sliced pickles can also be used for garnish.

Serve with pan-fried potatoes.

Our tip:
You can also prepare this dish with a whole beef roast. Preheat oven to 400 °F. Roast meat for approximately 75-85 min. Add chopped onions and julienne-sliced leek to roast after about 45 min.

F.Y.I.
"Zwiebelrostbraten" has been a traditional Viennese dish for centuries. When made with a generous amount of crushed garlic - once jokingly known as "the poor man's vanilla" - the result is a **"Vanillerost-braten."**

Esterhazy Steak or Beef Roast/ Esterhazy Rostbraten

4 sirloin steaks, approx. 7 oz each **or** 2 lbs beef tenderloin

black pepper

salt

2 - 3 T flour

4 - 5 T oil

9 oz fresh vegetables (e.g. 1 - 2 carrots, 1 small leek, 2 celery sticks)

1 medium onion

pinch of flour

pinch of sweet paprika powder

1/4 cup (2 oz) meat stock or water

juice of 1/2 lemon

1/2 cup (4 oz) sour cream

• Rinse steaks in cold water, pat dry with paper towel. Slash edges to prevent curling. Rub both sides of steak with salt and freshly ground black pepper. Dredge one side in flour, shake off excess.

• Heat oil in a large skillet. Sauté steaks, floured side first, at medium heat for 4-6 min. per side. Meat should still be pink inside (medium).

• Meanwhile, clean and finely slice carrots, leek, celery root and onions. Remove meat from skillet, place on warm platter and cover.

• Sauté vegetables in the same skillet. Season with paprika and dust with flour.

Add some broth or water and simmer until vegetables are tender. Add lemon juice and sour cream; remove skillet from heat. Return steaks to the skillet, let stand for several minutes and serve.

Our tip:
If you would like to make a roast instead of individual steaks, it takes approx. 75-85 min. to cook a 2-pound roast in a 425-450 °F oven. Add vegetables to roast after about

45 min. of cooking. Prepare sauce as described above.

F.Y.I.

"Whatever a king can do, I can do just as well," were famous words spoken by Field Marshal Esterhazy. At his lovely Esterhaza Castle in Hungary, he entertained many guests including Goethe, the famous German poet, and the composer Haydn.

29

Wiener Schnitzel/ Breaded Veal Cutlets

4 veal cutlets, approx. 6 - 7 oz each

2 eggs, beaten

2 T cream

salt, white pepper

approx. 1 cup (8 oz) oil

4 T flour

4 oz bread crumbs

softened butter

lemon slices and fresh parsley (garnish)

• Rinse the veal cutlets under cold water, pat dry with paper towel. Cut off any membrane or fat around edges to prevent curling. Pound cutlets on both sides with a cleaver. In a shallow bowl or pie pan, mix well eggs, cream, salt and pepper. Spread bread crumbs in a pie pan.

• Heat oil in a large skillet. Put flour on a plate, add salt and pepper, and dredge both sides of cutlets. Dip cutlets in egg mixture, then coat with bread crumbs.

• One after the other, place breaded cutlets in the hot oil over medium heat and fry for 3-5 min., turning occasionally. While cooking, carefully rotate the pan to ensure that the oil reaches all parts of the cutlets.

• When both sides are golden brown, remove from oil and drain on absorbent paper. You can also brush melted butter on the "schnitzel" before serving.

• Typically, Wiener Schnitzel is served with lemon wedges or slices and garnished with parsley.

Serve with Potato salad

F.Y.I.
Wiener Schnitzel is a classic of Viennese cuisine. It has become popular as such all over the world, even though it originates from Milan, Italy. Field Marshal Radetzky is said to have brought the recipe for "costoletta milanese" back to Vienna in 1848.

Styrian Root Vegetable Stew/ Steirisches Wurzelfleisch

approx. 2 lbs pork shoulder	2 - 4 celery sticks
1 large onion	1 large parsley root
salt	1 - 2 T vinegar
1 bay leaf	2 T butter
1/2 tsp peppercorns	2 T fresh grated horseradish
2 large carrots	

• Rinse pork shoulder in cold water, pat dry with absorbent paper and place in a large pot. Add hot water until meat is just covered. Bring to a boil, skim off the foam. Reduce heat and let simmer with cover on.

• Add coarsely chopped onions, bay leaf and black peppercorns to the simmering meat. Clean and peel carrots, celery root and parsley root. Coarsely chop half of vegetables and add to meat, cut remainder of vegetables into julienne strips. Set aside.

• Add vinegar to meat and simmer at low heat for about two hours. Then take meat out of broth. Strain broth. Cook julienned vegetables in butter and 1 - 2 cups of broth until vegetables are tender, but still crunchy.

• Cut cooked meat into slices or cubes and place in individual bowls. Add julienne vegetables and broth. Serve with freshly grated horseradish.

Our tip:
This dish goes well with boiled potatoes.

Fiaker Goulash/ Fiakergulasch

Vienna

approx. 2 lbs beef (for roasting)
approx. 1 1/2 lbs onions
2 T shortening or oil
2 T sweet paprika powder
1 T vinegar
approx. 3 cups (24 oz) beef stock
1 garlic clove, crushed
pinch of marjoram
1/2 tsp ground caraway
1 garlic clove, crushed
salt, pepper
1 T tomato paste
4 eggs
4 frankfurters
4 pickles (garnish)

• Rinse beef under cold water and pat dry with paper towel. Cut into large cubes. Peel onions and chop finely. Melt shortening in a large skillet and sauté onions until golden brown. Sprinkle with paprika powder; add vinegar and several tablespoons of beef stock.

• Add cubed meat and seasonings. Reduce heat, cover and simmer for about 1 1/2 hours, stirring frequently and adding stock as needed.

• When meat is tender, add remaining stock, tomato paste and crushed garlic. Simmer for 10 more min. and season to taste.

• Spoon goulash into soup bowls and garnish with a fried egg, frankfurter and a gherkin cut in fan-form.

Serve with Fresh white rolls,
steamed potatoes

F.Y.I.

The first official hackney driver
("Fiaker") was licensed in
Vienna in 1693. Today, the
few remaining genuine
coachers still wear their
traditional costume:
houndstooth trousers, velvet
jacket and top hat. Just as

unique is the goulash that
bears the Fiaker's name.
Goulash, or gulyas, originated
in Hungary. It is one of the few
dishes that actually improves
with time - it's even better as a
"leftover" than when freshly
prepared!

Szegediner Goulash/ Szegediner Gulasch

approx. 1 1/2 lbs loin or shoulder of pork	1 tsp sweet paprika powder
4 medium onions	approx. 1 lb sauerkraut
1 - 2 garlic cloves, crushed	1 T flour
approx. 2 oz shortening	1 cup (8 oz) sour cream
2 cups (3/4 pt) white veal stock or beef stock	1/2 tsp white pepper
	1/2 tsp salt
	ground caraway (optional)

• Rinse pork under cold water, pat dry with paper towel. Cut into 1 1/2-inch cubes.

• Peel onion and garlic, chop finely. Melt butter or shortening in a large pot and brown meat cubes over lively heat, stirring often. Add chopped onion and garlic until these become translucent.

• Add half of the veal stock to the meat-onion-garlic mixture. Simmer in open pot at low heat to reduce liquid. Sprinkle in paprika powder.

• Drain and rinse sauerkraut. Add to meat with remaining veal stock. Mix well. Continue simmering at low heat for 30-45 min. more, or until meat is tender, stirring occasionally. Beat flour into sour cream with a wire whisk. Add to goulash; simmer 10 min. more. Correct seasonings (salt, pepper, caraway).

Our tip:
Potato dumplings are the ideal accompaniment for this stew.

36

Austrian Meat Loaf/Faschierter Braten

approx. 1 1/4 lbs ground meat	1 T bread crumbs
1 medium onion	1 - 2 T stewed vegetables (optional)
2 T fresh parsley, finely chopped	2 slices of bacon
1 garlic clove, crushed	1 T butter
1/2 tsp pepper	1 medium onion
pinch of marjoram	1 medium carrot
pinch of nutmeg	1 T tomato paste
1 egg	2 T sour cream
salt	approx. 1 cup (8 oz) beef stock
1 dried white roll	1 T cornstarch

• Place ground meat in a large bowl. Finely chop onion and parsley. Sauté in butter until glassy, let cool and add to meat. Place a dried white roll or two slices of white bread in a cup of water until soft. Squeeze out excess water and add to meat, along with crushed garlic, pepper, marjoram, nutmeg, egg and bread crumbs. Knead well.

• Wet hands and form a long loaf with the meat mixture. To make a more decorative meat loaf, place layers of precooked vegetables (julienne carrots, green beans, peas, corn, etc.) between layers of meat in a loaf pan.

• Line a flat pan with bacon strips and place meat loaf on top. Bake in oven preheated to 400-425 °F.

• Somewhat later, baste meat loaf with melted butter. Cut onions into quarters, slice carrots and add to pan. Mix tomato paste with sour cream. Baste loaf with this mixture. Add stock to pan to keep loaf moist. Total baking time: 45-60 min.

• Take loaf from pan and let stand. Strain juice into another pan, bring to a boil and add cornstarch mixed with cold water to make a tasty gravy.

Stuffed Boneless Pork Rib Roast/
Gefüllte Schweinsbrust Salzburg

3 lbs pork breast	pinch of nutmeg
3/4 lb pork bones	2 T chopped onion
1/2 tsp salt	2 T finely chopped parsley
1/4 tsp pepper	1 oz softened butter
Stuffing:	1 T bread crumbs
3 dried white rolls or 3 slices dried white bread	**For roasting:**
2 eggs	2 oz shortening or oil
salt, pepper	1 onion, quartered
3 T cream	1 carrot, quartered
1/2 cup (4 oz) warm milk	2 cups (3/4 pt) hot beef stock
	3 - 4 T white wine
	2 T crème fraîche

• Ask your butcher to cut a long pocket in the roast, or cut one yourself. Season with salt and pepper inside and out.

• Stuffing: Cut bread into cubes. Lightly beat eggs with heavy cream, milk and seasonings. Pour over diced bread. Sauté minced onions and parsley in butter. Add to bread and let stand about 30 min. Add bread crumbs to thicken. Fill the roast cavity with the stuffing and sew closed. Preheat oven to 400-425 °F.

• Heat shortening in a roasting pan. Brown both sides of the roast, along with carrots, quartered onions and soup bones. Cover with about 1 cup of stock. Place roaster in oven and reduce heat to 350-375 °F. Roasting time: approximately 2 hours. Baste occasionally.

• When tender, remove roast from oven to warmed platter. Bring pan drippings to a boil, put in a blender or through a sieve. Add white wine and again bring to a boil.

• Remove from heat and add crème fraîche. Remove thread from roast, slice and serve. Serve sauce separately.

Delicious with green peas and carrots.

Smoked Ham in Sourdough/ Bauerngeselchtes in Brotteig

Lower Austria

| 3 lbs smoked ham |
| 8 cups (2 qts) water |
| 9 oz fresh vegetables (e.g. 1 - 2 medium onions, 1 small leek, 2 celery sticks, 1/2 parsley root) |
| 2 - 3 T parsley, finely chopped |
| 3 lbs bread dough (whole grain) |
| 2 egg yolks, beaten with |
| 2 T milk |

• Soak ham in cold water for 24 hours. Place in a large pot and cover with hot water. Add coarsely chopped root vegetables, bring to a boil and simmer gently for about 1 hour. Remove ham roast and pat dry with absorbent paper.

• Roll dough out on a floured surface to form a rectangle about 1/2-inch in thickness. Place ham on dough, bring long sides up around roast and then ends. Prick holes in dough using a fork. Place dough-covered roast on baking pan covered with baking paper.

• Beat egg yolks with milk and brush on dough. Let stand for

about 30 min. Bake in a 350-
375 °F oven for about 2 hours.
Let cool for 90 min., slice and
serve.

Serve with: Creamy
horseradish sauce, salad.

F.Y.I.
Every farm has its own

"secret" recipe for smoke-
curing meats. Ten to twenty-
pound pieces of pork are
rubbed with a mixture of salt,
garlic, sugar, coriander and
caraway, placed in a wooden
vat and stored in a cool place
for about 10 days before
smoking.

Fried Chicken/ Backhendl

Vienna

2 small chickens, approx. 2 lbs each
2 eggs, lightly beaten
2 T cream
salt, white pepper
pinch of sweet paprika powder
4 oz flour
5 oz bread crumbs
9 oz shortening **or** 1/2 cup oil
2 lemon wedges or slices
parsley to garnish

• Clean and quarter fresh chicken, rinse under cold water and pat dry with absorbent paper. Remove skin; remove ribs and cartilage from breast pieces. Beat eggs, heavy cream, salt, pepper and paprika in a small, deep bowl. Put flour and bread crumbs on separate plates.

• Lightly salt chicken pieces. First dredge in flour and shake off excess. Then dip in egg batter until completely coated. Finally, dredge in bread crumbs. Shake off excess crumbs.

• Heat oil or shortening slowly in a heavy, deep skillet. Place breaded chicken pieces in oil and fry for 10-15 min., until

golden brown. Gently lift and rotate the pan to ensure that oil reaches all parts of the chicken.

• Remove chicken pieces and drain on absorbent paper. If you need to keep chicken warm, cover with aluminum foil or place in warm oven. To serve, place on warmed platter. Garnish with lemon wedges and parsley.

Potato salad, optionally garnished with sliced cucumber, is an ideal **side dish.**

Deep-Fried Carp/ Gebackener Karpfen

1 carp, approx. 3 lbs
salt, pepper
fresh lemon juice
2 eggs
4 oz (1/2 cup) flour
5 oz (2/3 cup) bread crumbs
approx. 1 cup (8 oz) oil

• Clean and rinse carp. Cut into four equal pieces. Season with salt, pepper and lemon juice. Let stand for 10-15 min. Beat eggs. Place flour and bread crumbs on separate plates. Dredge fish pieces in flour, dip in egg, then dredge in bread crumbs. Shake off excess crumbs.

• Heat oil in a deep pan. Place breaded fish in oil and fry for 6-8 min. per side, until golden brown. Drain on absorbent paper and serve immediately.

Tyrolean Bacon Dumplings/
Tiroler Speckknödel

9 oz bacon

5 oz smoked sausage **or** ham

6 - 7 slices of dried white bread **or** 6 - 7 dried white rolls

3 eggs, lightly beaten

4 oz (1/2 cup) milk

1 T softened butter

approx. 3 T flour

1 T parsley, finely chopped

1 T chives, finely chopped

salt, pepper

• Cut bacon and sausage into small cubes. Sauté and let cool. Add to diced bread or plain croutons. Beat eggs and milk; pour over bread. Add butter, flour, parsley and chives. Season to taste with salt and pepper. Mix well and let stand for about 20 min.

• Fill large pot with salted water; bring to a boil. Wet hands and form eight 2 1/2-inch dumplings. Gently drop dumplings into hot water, turn heat down very low and simmer for 12-15 min. Remove dumplings, drain and serve.

Cabbage Strudel/ Krautstrudel

Burgenland

Dough:

9 oz flour	
1 egg	
1 T oil	
salt	
3 oz (1/3 cup) water	

Filling:

1 large onion	
approx. 2 lbs white cabbage	
5 T butter	
pinch of sugar	
1 - 2 T white wine	
approx. 4 oz (1/2 cup) meat stock	
salt, white pepper	
pinch of ground caraway	
4 oz (1/2 cup) cream	
2 - 3 oz butter	
flour (for work surface)	

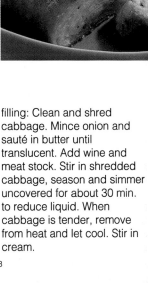

• Dough: Sift flour into a bowl. Make a depression in the middle and drop in egg, oil and salt. Add water gradually while slowly beating the dough until it forms a solid ball. Knead by hand for 10 more min., until the dough has a sheen. Let stand about 30 min.

• Meanwhile, prepare the filling: Clean and shred cabbage. Mince onion and sauté in butter until translucent. Add wine and meat stock. Stir in shredded cabbage, season and simmer uncovered for about 30 min. to reduce liquid. When cabbage is tender, remove from heat and let cool. Stir in cream.

Spread a large dishtowel or sheet on a table, dust with flour and roll dough out very thinly. Grease a cookie sheet and preheat oven to 375-410 °F.

Melt butter. Brush half of butter onto strudel dough. Spread cabbage filling evenly over dough. Lift one side of cloth and without touching the dough, roll the dough over onto itself jelly-roll fashion, until the filling is completely enclosed. Carefully fold over ends and use cloth to transfer strudel to the cookie sheet. Brush remaining butter on rolled strudel and bake for 50-60 min., until golden brown.

Carinthian Cheese Pastries/
Kärntner Kasnudeln

Dough:

11 oz (1 1/2 cups) flour, pinch of salt

oil, 1 egg, approx. 2 T water

Filling:

5 oz salad potatoes

11 oz curd **or** cottage cheese

2 - 3 T sour cream

2 T mixed herbs

pinch of white pepper, nutmeg

1 egg white, 3 oz butter

2 T parsley, finely chopped

• Combine flour, egg, salt and some water to form a not too soft pasta dough. I recommend using an electric mixer with dough hooks. Brush the finished dough with a few drops of oil and let stand for about 30 min.

• Rice the boiled, skinned potatoes. Combine with drained cheese, cream, herbs and spices. Blend thoroughly.

• Roll dough out thinly on a floured surface. Cut out 4-inch circles using a cookie cutter or large glass. Place a tablespoon of filling on the dough circle, brush edges with egg white, fold and press edges tightly together.

• Cook pastries in boiling salted water for 10-14 min. Remove from water, drain and serve with brown butter and chopped parsley.

Stuffed Dumplings from the Mühlviertel/ Mühlviertler G'hackknödel

Upper Austria

Dumpling dough:

1 1/4 lbs potatoes

salt, water

Filling:

4 oz roast pork

4 oz roast beef

5 oz pork sausage meat

1 medium onion

1 garlic clove, crushed

salt, white pepper

pinch of marjoram

1 - 2 T butter

• Dough: Mix flour, water and salt into a light dough. Roll out to about 1/4-inch thickness. Use cookie cutter or glass to cut 2-inch circles.

• Filling: Mince cooked pork, beef and sausage (use a meat grinder). Add minced onions and garlic. Season to taste with salt, pepper and marjoram. Use a teaspoon to form walnut-sized scoops, place on dough circles and roll into dumplings. Drop dumplings into boiling salted water, turn heat down low and cook for 15-20 min., or until dumplings rise. Remove with a slotted spoon. Drizzle with melted butter and serve.

Tyrolean Pan-Fried Potatoes/ Tiroler Gröstl

approx. 1 1/2 lbs potatoes, cooked	salt, white pepper
1 large onion	1 tsp marjoram
12 oz roast pork	2 - 3 T parsley, coarsely chopped
5 oz smoked sausage **or** ham	4 eggs
3 oz shortening **or** 4 T oil	butter or margarine (for frying)

• Peel boiled potatoes and slice (leftover boiled potatoes also work well). Peel and finely chop onions. Cut pork roast and sausage into thin, bite-sized slices.

• Heat shortening in a skillet and sauté onions until translucent. Stir in potatoes and meat; fry, turning ingredients occasionally. Reduce heat and fry for 10-15 min. more. Season with salt, pepper and marjoram.

• Chop parsley and sprinkle over potatoes when serving. Often served with a fried egg.

Our tip:
Tyrolean Gröstl goes well with Austrian-style cole slaw, which is made with hot bacon dressing.

F.Y.I.
Genuine Tyrolean Gröstl is made with roast pork. If you use leftover beef, you then have "Farmer's Gröstl." Add sautéed veal to the potatoes and you have "Innsbruck-style Gröstl," also known as "Gentleman's Gröstl." Use approx. 1 lb meat and somewhat less potatoes when making the latter.

Cheese Spaetzle/Kässpätzle

Vorarlberg

1 1/2 lbs flour	9 oz grated cheese (Swiss and Gruyère)
3 eggs, lightly beaten	
1/4 tsp salt	6 oz butter
approx. 2 cups water	2 - 3 large onions

• Beat flour, egg, salt and water until smooth. Drop small bits of the batter from a spoon or through a colander into simmering salted water. Simmer until done, about 1-3 min. Drain immediately.

• Coarsely grate cheese. Layer with spaetzle in a deep pie dish or bowl. End with a layer of cheese. Keep warm.

• Melt butter in a large skillet. Slice onions into thin rings and fry until golden brown. Drain and use to garnish spaetzle.

Austrian Pastries and Desserts

Austria's pastries and sweet dishes are known all over the world. Even though some of the sweet, as well as savory, pastries can be eaten as entrées, Austrians and particularly the Viennese prefer them as desserts or for afternoon tea.

In any case, each delicious dish is based on flour made of wheat or some other grain. Every province boasts its own delicious specialties. Some of these have gained world renown, such as the Viennese Apple Strudel, "Salzburger Nockerln," "Linzer Torte," and "Sacher Torte."

Not only flour, but also baker's cheese, eggs and milk play important roles in the various recipes. Stewed fruits and sauces provide minerals and vitamins. These dishes are therefore quite nutritious.

Typical pastries and desserts include the strudels, pancake dishes, dumplings - both plain and fruit-filled - Austrian crêpes ("Palatschinken") and yeast-based sweets.

One distinct advantage of all these recipes is that almost all are made with high-quality, low-cost, readily accessible ingredients. Nor do you need any special kitchen tools to make these treats.

Whenever recipes call for beaten egg whites, these must be very stiff. This can be accomplished by adding several drops of lemon juice.

Cheese Crêpes/ Topfen-palatschinken

Batter:

7 oz flour, sifted
2 eggs
pinch of salt
2 oz sugar
12 oz (1 1/2 cups) cold milk
3 oz butter (for frying)

Filling:

2 oz raisins
1 T rum
1 - 2 oz softened butter
4 oz sugar
1/2 tsp vanilla extract
grated rind of 1/2 lemon
2 eggs
9 oz curd, baker's cheese **or** cottage cheese
2 T powdered sugar, sifted (for decoration)

• To make batter, sift flour, add 3 tablespoons milk, eggs, salt and sugar. With an electric mixer, beat to form a thin, smooth batter, adding milk as necessary. Let stand about 20 min. Melt butter in a medium-sized skillet. Ladle in about 1/8 of the batter and tip the pan to let the batter spread over the bottom of the pan, keeping the pan moving. Bake golden brown at low heat; when batter edges pull away from pan, turn pancake. Batter makes 8 golden-brown pancakes. Place on a platter, cover and keep warm.

• Filling: Stew raisins until soft, drain and mix with rum. Cream butter with sugar,

vanilla and grated lemon rind.
Separate eggs and add yolks.
Mix in drained cheese or
creamed cottage cheese and
raisins. Beat egg whites until
stiff and fold gently into
mixture.

• Spread cottage cheese
mixture onto pancakes, roll,
sprinkle with powdered sugar
and serve.

F.Y.I.
Palatschinken have been a
staple of Viennese cuisine
since the 19th century. These
thin pancakes originated in
Romania, where they were
called "placinta" or "flat
cakes." The Hungarians
changed the name to
"palacinta." When these
delicious pancakes arrived in
Vienna, they became
"palatschinken."

Apple Strudel/ Apfelstrudel

Strudel dough:

7 oz flour, sifted
1 egg, lightly beaten
1 T oil
pinch of salt
approx. 3 oz (1/3 cup) water

Filling:

3 oz raisins
2 T rum
2 oz butter, softened
3 1/2 lbs cooking apples
4 oz sugar
pinch of cinnamon
3 - 4 oz (1/2 cup) bread crumbs
approx. 4 oz butter, softened
2 - 3 T powdered sugar, sifted (for decoration)

• Dough: Sift flour into a bowl. Make a depression in the middle and drop in egg, oil and salt. Add water gradually while slowly beating the dough until it forms a medium-firm ball. Knead by hand for 10 min. more, until the dough has a silky sheen. Let stand about 30 min.

• Filling: Drizzle rum over raisins and let stand. Peel and seed apples, slice thinly. Stir in cinnamon and sugar.

• Spread a clean tablecloth or sheet on a large table. Sprinkle with flour and roll dough out as thin as possible. Stretch the dough gently from the center out using the backs of your hands, lightly clenched, palms down,

moving around the table. Cut off thicker edges and use to patch if necessary.

• Preheat oven to 400-425 °F. Grease baking sheet. Sprinkle bread crumbs on dough. Cover 2/3 of the dough with apple filling and raisins. Fold sides of dough in over filling. Using the cloth, gently roll dough over itself, jelly-roll fashion, until filling is enclosed. Use cloth to slide strudel onto baking sheet. Baste with melted butter. Bake for 45-55 min., basting occasionally with butter. Dust with powdered sugar before serving.

Variation:

Add sunflower seeds instead of raisins.

Emperor's Pancake/ Kaiserschmarrn

Vienna

2 oz raisins
2 - 3 T rum
5 oz flour
pinch of salt
1 T powdered sugar, sifted
1/2 tsp vanilla extract
grated rind of 1/2 lemon
3 egg yolks, lightly beaten
3 egg whites
4 oz (1/2 cup) milk
1 tsp lemon juice
2 oz ground almonds (optional)
2 - 3 oz butter or margarine
2 T powdered sugar, sifted (for decoration)

• Stew raisins, drain and drizzle with rum. Sift flour into large bowl. Beat in salt, powdered sugar, vanilla, grated lemon rind, egg yolks and milk, until smooth. Let stand 20-30 min.

• Beat egg whites with powdered sugar and a few drops of lemon juice until very stiff. If desired, add ground almonds. Fold whites into batter.

• Melt butter in a large skillet. Pour in batter, sprinkle with raisins. Cover. Heat until underside is golden brown. Turn. Using two forks, gently pull pancake into bite-sized pieces and complete cooking,

stirring and turning pieces often. Serve hot, sprinkled generously with powdered sugar.

Our tip:
Serve "Kaiserschmarrn" with cranberries, apple sauce or stewed fruits. Eat as a main dish or, in smaller portions, as dessert.

F.Y.I.
According to legend, the court chef dedicated this dish to Empress Elizabeth, wife of Austrian Emperor Franz Josef I, calling it the "Empress Pancake" (Kaiserinschmarrn). Since it was not to her liking, but instead satisfied the Emperor's sweet tooth, it was simply renamed.

Apricot Dumplings from the Wachau/ Wachauer Marillenknödel

approx. 1 lb salad potatoes, cooked

pinch of salt,4 - 5 oz flour

2 T semolina, 1 1/2 oz butter

2 egg yolks

1 tsp grated lemon rind

Filling:

1 lb fresh apricots

5 - 6 sugar cubes

4 oz brown butter, mixed with sugar and

4 oz (1/2 cup) bread crumbs

• Boil, peel and rice mature baking potatoes. Let cool. Combine in a large bowl with salt, flour, semolina, butter, egg yolks and grated lemon rind to form a smooth dough. Let stand for approx. 30 min.

• Wash apricots and press out pits. Replace each pit with 1 sugar cube. Roll dough out into a 2 1/2-inch-thick sausage; cut into 3/4-inch-thick slices. Flatten each slice somewhat and place apricot in center. Dust your hands with flour and fold dough over fruit. Roll gently until entire apricot is covered with dough.

• Gently drop dumplings into simmering salted water. Bring to a boil, then reduce heat. While dumplings are simmering (2-5 min.), lightly

brown the bread crumbs in melted butter. Remove skillet from heat. Remove dumplings with a slotted spoon, rinse quickly in cold water and roll in bread crumbs. Place dumplings on plates and dust with powdered sugar. Serve immediately.

Yeast Dumplings/ Germknödel

9 oz (1 cup and 1 T) flour

1/4 cup (2 oz) milk

1 oz fresh yeast **or** 1 T (1/2 pkg) dried yeast, plus 1 tsp sugar

pinch of salt

1 egg yolk

1 oz butter, softened

4 oz plum jam, 1 tsp rum

pinch of cinnamon

2 oz ground poppy seeds

2 1/2 oz powdered sugar, sifted

2 1/2 oz brown butter

• Sift flour into large bowl. In separate bowl, blend lukewarm milk, yeast and sugar; add to flour. Add salt, egg yolk and soft butter. Beat with dough hooks until smooth. Cover and let rise in a warm place for about 45 min.
• Mix plum jam with rum and cinnamon. Divide dough into 4 - 6 equal pieces. Put one teaspoon of prune filling in the middle of each piece, fold dough over filling and roll in

floured hands to form dumplings. Let rise for 20 min. Simmer dumplings in salted water over low heat, turning after about 6-8 min. (total time: 12-16 min.). Drain gently, serve and place on plates. Sprinkle with ground poppy seeds and powdered sugar; drizzle with brown butter.

Plum Pockets/ Powidltascherln

Potato dough:
See "Apricot Dumplings"

Filling:
5 oz plum jam

1 - 2 tsp sugar

pinch of cinnamon

2 T rum, 1 egg white

2 oz melted butter

3 T bread crumbs

2 T powdered sugar, sifted (for decoration)

• Make dough as described above for Apricot Dumplings. Mix plum jam with cinnamon and sugar. Roll dough out on a floured surface to about 1/4-inch thickness. Cut out circles about 3 inches in diameter. Place a teaspoon of prune filling in the center of each circle and brush edges with egg white. Fold over and press edges firmly together. Simmer in salted water for 7-9 min. Brown bread crumbs in butter; remove skillet from heat. Transfer pockets from water to skillet with a slotted spoon; shake pan to cover pockets. Sprinkle with powdered sugar before serving.

Poppy Seed Dumplings/ Mohnnudeln

Potato dough:
See "Apricot Dumplings"

flour for work surface

Topping:
2 1/2 oz butter

4 oz ground poppy seeds

2 - 3 T powdered sugar, sifted (for decoration)

• Make dough as described above for Apricot Dumplings. Bring large pot of salted water to a boil. Roll the dough into a long 1 1/2-thick oblong. Cut off walnut-sized pieces and roll these out into cigar-shaped cylinders, pointed at both ends. Drop into water and simmer for 6-8 min.

• In a skillet, stir ground poppy seeds into melted butter. Transfer dumplings to skillet with a slotted spoon and rotate to coat dumplings with poppy seed butter. Serve with powdered sugar.

Cheese Dumplings with Plums/ **Topfenknödel**

18 oz curd, baker's cheese **or** cottage cheese

4 eggs

4 1/2 oz (1/2 cup) bread crumbs

4 oz (2/3 cup) sugar

pinch of salt

1/2 tsp vanilla extract

4 oz (1/2 cup) bread crumbs, roasted in

2 1/2 oz butter

1 lb fresh **or** canned plums

2 T sugar, pinch of cinnamon

1 T rum, 1 tsp lemon juice

• Drain cottage cheese and press through a sieve. Mix with eggs, bread crumbs, sugar, salt and vanilla extract until smooth. Let stand for about 45 min.

• With wet hands, form 2-inch dumplings. Drop into boiling salted water, reduce heat and simmer gently for about 10 min. Brown bread crumbs in butter in a skillet. Transfer dumplings to skillet with slotted spoon and rotate gently to coat dumplings.

• Wash plums and cut in half, removing pits. In a small skillet, cook plums with sugar, cinnamon, rum and lemon juice. Serve separately.

Salzburger Nockerln with Cassis Sauce

• Preheat oven to 400-425 °F. Combine butter, cream, vanilla extract and sugar in a pot and bring to a boil, beating constantly with a wire whisk. Remove from heat. Beat egg yolks and sugar until fluffy. Add white wine, sifted flour and salt and continue beating until batter is very creamy.

• In a separate bowl, beat egg whites until very stiff (if necessary, add several drops of lemon juice). Fold quickly into egg yolk mixture. Butter and dust with powdered sugar a large, straight-sided ovenproof baker. Gently transfer batter to form 3 mounds. Place in oven immediately and bake for 12-16 min., or until golden brown.

• While soufflé is baking, prepare cassis sauce by

1 1/2 oz butter	
4 oz (1/2 cup) cream	
1/2 tsp vanilla extract	
4 egg yolks	
3 oz sugar	
2 T white wine	
1 1/2 oz flour	
pinch of salt	
8 egg whites	
2 T powdered sugar, sifted	

Sauce:

5 T black currant jelly	
4 oz (1/2 cup) red wine	
1 T honey	
1 tsp sugar, mixed with	
1/4 tsp vanilla extract	

heating currant jelly with red wine, honey and vanilla extract. Bring to a boil and stir vigorously. Spoon soufflé onto individual plates, dust generously with powdered sugar and drizzle with cassis sauce.

Our tip:
It is very important to preheat the oven to ensure that this very fragile dessert bakes

quickly. Do not open the oven door while soufflé is baking, or it might collapse.

F.Y.I.
Salzburger Nockerln are considered the prima donna of Austrian desserts. According to history, this delicate soufflé was first served in the 16th century.

Apple Fritters/ Apfelschöberl

Burgenland

4 oz (1/2 cup) milk	
2 eggs, pinch of salt	
5 oz (1/2 cup) flour	
3 - 4 baking apples	
butter or margarine for frying	
1 T sugar	

• Blend milk, eggs, salt and flour to make a thick batter. Peel and cut apples into 3/4-inch-thick slices or wedges. Dip in batter and immediately

fry in butter or shortening until golden brown.

• Remove, drain and sprinkle with sugar.

Our tip:
Using this same technique and recipe, you can make fritters with elderberry blossoms, as well as with apricot, pear or peach wedges.

Cream Strudel/Milirahmstrudel

Lower Austria

Strudel dough:

See "Apple Strudel"

Filling:

5 - 6 slices of dried white bread **or** 5 - 6 dried white rolls

8 oz (1 cup) warm milk

4 1/2 oz butter

4 1/2 oz powdered sugar, sifted

juice of 1/2 lemon

4 eggs, pinch of salt

1 cup (8 oz) sour cream

3 oz raisins

2 1/2 oz butter

approx. 1 cup (8 oz) hot milk

• Cut crusts off dried bread. Soak in milk, press excess milk out and pass through a sieve. Blend butter with sugar, lemon juice, egg yolks and salt. Stir in bread mass and sour cream. Whip egg whites until stiff; fold into batter.

• Spread batter onto strudel dough. Scatter with raisins and roll jelly-roll fashion. Place in a greased pan, brush with melted butter and bake in a 400-425 °F. oven for 50-60 min. After the first 20-25 min. of baking, pour hot milk over strudel.

Linzer Torte

5 oz (2/3 cup) flour

5 oz (2/3 cup) ground almonds

5 oz (2/3 cup) sugar

1/4 tsp vanilla essence

pinch of salt

1 tsp cinnamon

pinch of powdered cloves

grated rind of 1 lemon

4 egg yolks

5 oz butter, softened

7 oz black currant jelly

2 oz almond slivers

butter and bread crumbs or ground almonds for the baking pan

1 T powdered sugar, sifted (for decoration)

• Sift flour into a large bowl. Stir in ground almonds, sugar, vanilla, salt, cinnamon, ground cloves and grated lemon rind. Add 3 egg yolks and cold butter, cut into thin pats. Work into a soft, rich dough. Cover and refrigerate for about 30 min.

• Preheat oven to 340-375 °F. Butter a 9-inch spring form, coat with bread crumbs if desired. Distribute 2/3 of dough evenly in the form, about 1/4-inch thick. Spread currant marmalade over dough, leaving a 1/2-inch edge free. Roll out half of remaining dough into thin strips. Weave a lattice over the marmalade. Use the rest of the dough to form an edge around the torte. Brush with remaining egg yolk and

sprinkle with shaved almond
slivers. Bake for 45-50 min.,
until golden brown. Let cool
and dust with powdered
sugar.

Our tip:
Linzer tortes can be prepared
well in advance. To store,
simply wrap in aluminum foil.
Instead of currant jam, many
Austrians also use cranberry
preserves.

Sacher Torte

5 oz butter	
4 oz powdered sugar, sifted	
8 egg yolks	
5 oz dark chocolate	
5 oz (2/3 cup) flour	
8 egg whites	
2 oz sugar	
2 T apricot jam	
8 oz (1 cup) cream	
4 oz dark chocolate glaze	

• Cream softened butter and powdered sugar. Beat in egg yolks one after another until the mixture is thick and creamy. Melt bittersweet chocolate in a double boiler or microwave oven. Stir melted chocolate until lukewarm, then stir into cream by the teaspoonful. Sift in flour.

Beat egg whites with sugar until stiff. Gently fold into chocolate mixture with a wire whisk.

• Line bottom of 9-inch spring form pan with baking paper circle. Spread batter evenly and bake in a 340-375 °F oven for 50-65 min. Remove and let cool for several minutes. Run a knife around the cake and remove sides of pan. Let cake cool completely on wire rack. Remove paper and, if necessary, even out cake bottom with a knife.

- Stir and warm apricot preserves. Smooth over entire cake, including sides.

- Melt commercial chocolate glaze to frost cake. Decorate as desired. Serve with whipped cream.

F.Y.I.

This recipe, though typical, is not the one for the "Original Sacher Torte," which is a heavily guarded secret of the Sacher Company. In the peak season, over 2000 tasty tortes are produced each day by Sacher, Vienna, ready for export to all corners of the world.

Austrian Coffee Ring/ Guglhupf

14 oz (1 3/4 cups) flour	5 eggs
4 oz (1/2 cup) ground almonds	pinch of salt
1 1/2 oz fresh yeast **or** 2 T (1 pkg) dried yeast, plus 1 T sugar	4 oz (1/2 cup) cream
	3 oz raisins, 4 T rum
4 oz (1/2 cup) lukewarm milk	grated rind of 1 lemon
5 oz (2/3 cup) sugar	butter and bread crumbs or ground almonds for the baking pan
5 oz butter	1 T powdered sugar, sifted

• Blend sifted flour with ground almonds in a large bowl. Make a depression in the middle. Crumble in compressed yeast, lukewarm milk and several teaspoons of sugar. Stir and let rise in a warm place for about 15 min.

• Preheat oven to 350-400 °F. Melt butter and beat with remaining sugar, eggs, salt and cream until very light and creamy.

• Stir in raisins, rum and grated lemon rind. Add this mixture to the yeast dough and beat well until smooth and elastic. Batter should pull away from the sides of the bowl.

• Grease a 9-inch fluted tube pan and dust with bread crumbs. Pour in dough and bake for 45-60 min.

• Let cake cool in the pan. Turn it over onto a wire rack and dust top with powdered sugar.

F.Y.I.
Fluted "Guglhupf" forms are reminiscent of the sun's rays. Some of the earliest pans were found in Roman excavations dating back to 300 A.D.

Cheese and Plum Cake/ Topfen-Zwetschgen-Kuchen

13 oz (1 2/3 cups) flour	3 egg yolks
1 1/2 oz fresh yeast **or** 2 T (1 pkg) dried yeast, plus 1 T sugar	1 T grated lemon rind
	2 T cornstarch
4 oz (1/2 cup) lukewarm milk	4 oz (1/2 cup) cream
1 egg	2 lbs curd, baker's cheese **or** cottage cheese
2 oz (1/4 cup) sugar	
pinch of salt	3 egg whites
1/4 tsp vanilla extract	2 - 3 lbs fresh plums
2 oz butter	butter for baking pan
Topping:	ground almonds (for decoration)
4 1/2 oz (1/2 cup) sugar	

• Mix together flour, crumbled yeast, lukewarm milk, egg, sugar, salt, vanilla extract and softened butter in a large bowl to form a soft dough. Let rise in a warm place for about 20 min.

• Topping: Beat sugar, egg yolks and grated lemon rind until foamy. Add cornstarch and cream. Drain cottage cheese, pass through a sieve, add to egg batter and continue beating until batter is smooth and creamy. Beat egg whites until stiff and fold gently into egg mixture.

• Wash plums, cut in half and remove pits. Grease baking sheet and spread dough evenly. Dust with ground almonds and prick in several places with a fork. Spread cottage cheese mixture over the top. Press plum halves, skin down, gently into the batter.

• If desired, sprinkle with additional sugar. Bake at 400-425 °F for 30-45 min.

Cherry Pockets/Kirschmandel-tascherln

Potato dough:

See "Apricot Dumplings"

9 oz fresh or canned cherries

4 oz (1/2 cup) sugar

2 qts water

1 1/2 oz butter

2 tsp flour

some milk

1 egg white

2 oz butter

3 T bread crumbs

1 T powdered sugar, sifted (for decoration)

• Wash cherries and remove pits. Boil with sugar and some water. In a saucepan, make a roux of flour and butter, add a few teaspoons of milk. Boil to thicken, stirring constantly. Add to cherries as a binder.

• Prepare potato dough, roll out thinly and cut 2 1/2-inch circles. Brush edges with egg white. Place a teaspoonful of cherry mixture in center, fold dough over to make pocket and press edges together tightly.

Bring 2 qts of salted water to a boil, gently drop in pockets and reduce heat. Simmer gently for 7-9 min. Remove pockets and drain. Brown bread crumbs in butter in skillet; add pockets and coat with bread crumbs.

Coffee Primer

When you order a cup of coffee in Munich or Paris, you'll get one quickly and without much ado. In Austria, however, coffee is more than a mere beverage: it is a tradition. Coffee is best enjoyed in one of Austria's countless coffeehouses. Enjoyment requires peace and quiet, and coffeehouses offer so much of it that it's even possible to read a newspaper without being constantly interrupted by a waiter requesting further orders. The waiter will only refill the mandatory glass of water without being asked.

In Austria, particularly Vienna, coffee is served in myriad ways. I would like to tell you about some of these specialties:

A **"Pharisäer"** (German for Pharisee), with its whipped cream cap, might look innocent, but be prepared - it's made with a large shot of rum. The **"Konsul"** (or consul) doesn't have anything to do with diplomacy; it consists of black coffee with a dash of cream. An **"Einspänner"** (one-horse carriage) is a

double mocha, served in a tall glass with lots of whipped cream and topped with powdered sugar. After a good meal, a cup of Turkish coffee is preferred. Other Viennese coffee specialties are the **Maria Theresa Coffee,** which contains orange liqueur, and the **"Kaiser-Melange"** (Imperial Melange) with an egg yolk. The Austrian **"Kapuziner"** (capuccino) is made with strong espresso coffee, topped with whipped cream and dusted with cocoa powder.

The "kleiner Braune" (small espresso) and "grosser Braune" (large espresso) are two versions of coffee and cream. If some happens to be left over, let it cool, mix in some maraschino liqueur, pour over ice in a fancy glass and you have a **"Mazagran."**

If you would like to offer your guests **"Kaffee mit Schleppe,"** you must provide an appealing dessert or pastry with the coffee.

About the Recipes:

Most recipes serve four. The desserts and pastries, since they may also be served as main dishes, can serve more. Oven temperatures are given for ovens with top and bottom heat. If you use a convection oven, reduce heat by about 50 °F. Baking times remain the same.

Guide to Abbreviations:

I have used the following abbreviations or terms in this book:

lb	pound
min.	minute(s)
oz	ounce(s)
pt	pint
qt	quart
T	tablespoon(s)
tsp	teaspoon(s)

Upper Austrian Power Plant AG Photo Archives, Linz: pages 3, 5, 6, 12, 13, 14, 29, 51, 54, 65, 72.
Fotostudio Teubner, Füssen: pages 33, 36.
Komplettbüro GmbH, Munich: pages 15, 16, 17, 19, 20, 25, 38, 41, 43, 44, 47, 48, 59, 68, 77.
Vitri-Corning GmbH, Mühltal: pages 27, 75.
Eskimo-Iglo GmbH, Vienna: pages 64/65, 69, 78.
Austrian Tourism Promotion, Vienna: pages 31, 44.

The author and publishing company would like to express their thanks to the above organizations for providing an excellent assortment of photographic material and other assistance.
English translation by: Mary Heaney MARGREITER

Photo credits:

Front cover: Fotostudio Teubner, Füssen
Back cover: Sigloch Edition, Künzelsau
Sigloch Edition, Künzelsau: pages 10, 22, 34, 47, 50, 53, 56, 61.

Publishing Number: 1718
ISBN 3-85491-811-9

©**KOMPASS-Karten GmbH Rum/Innsbruck**
Fax 0043 (0) 512/265561-8
e-mail: kompass@kompass.at
http://www.kompass.at
4th Edition 2002